The Tree Frog

First Steck-Vaughn Edition 1992

This book has been reviewed
for accuracy by
David Skryja
Associate Professor of Biology
University of Wisconsin Center—Waukesha.

Library of Congress Cataloging in Publication Data

Oda, Hidetomo.
  The tree frog.

  (Nature close-ups)
  Translation of: Amagaeru / text by Hidetomo Oda,
photographs by Atsushi Sakurai.
  Summary: Discusses the life cycle and behavior
patterns of tree frogs.
  1. Hylidae—Juvenile literature.   [1. Tree frogs.
2. Frogs]   I. Sakurai, Atsushi, ill.   II. Title.
III. Series.
QL668.E2403513   1986   597.8′7   85-28194

ISBN 0-8172-2546-3 (lib. bdg.)
ISBN 0-8172-2571-4 (softcover)

This edition first published in 1986 by Raintree Publishers Inc.,
a Division of Steck-Vaughn Company.

Text copyright © 1986 by Raintree Publishers Inc., translated by Jun
Amano from *Tree Frog* copyright © 1976 by Jun Nanao and
Hidetomo Oda.

Photographs copyright © 1976 by Atsushi Sakurai.

World English translation rights for *Color Photo Books on Nature*
arranged with Kaisei-Sha through Japan Foreign-Rights Center.

2 3 4 5 6 7 8 9 0   95 94 93 92 91

The Tree Frog

RAINTREE
STECK-VAUGHN
L I B R A R Y
A Division of Steck-Vaughn Company

An oak tree in early summer.

Tree frogs are hard to spot on trees because they are very small and because they blend in with the color of the trees. Often, people can hear tree frogs but cannot see them.

▶ **A tree frog singing in the rain.**

In some countries, people believe frogs can foretell when it is going to rain. And some people believe a frog's singing can actually make it rain.

On an early spring night, after the first warm rain of the year, a chorus of sound breaks the stillness of the evening. Hundreds of frogs, just awakened from their winter's hibernation, have gathered at the edge of ponds and lakes and puddles to sing their mating songs.

Of the more than 2,500 kinds, or species, of frogs in the world, tree frogs are among the most beautiful singers. Of those species of tree frogs which live in the United States, people are probably most familiar with the spring peeper. Its clear piping music, which resembles the sound of sleigh bells, can be heard a mile or more away.

◀ **A tree frog in a marsh.**

Tree frogs usually live in trees or bushes, except in the spring. Then they hop to the nearest source of water, in order to mate.

▶ **A male frog singing.**

The vocal sac beneath its chin inflates as this frog sings. Some species of frogs have two vocal sacs, one on each side of the head.

Male frogs instinctively hop to ponds or streams because female frogs lay their eggs in water. Often a dozen or more different kinds of frogs gather at the same place. When one frog begins to sing, the others join in, as if they are competing with one another. Each species has its own song, and, in most species, only the male sings. When a female of the same species hears the male, she responds by following the sound.

When a frog sings, it inhales air through its nostrils and then closes its nostrils and mouth, trapping the air inside. The air passes back and forth over the vocal chords and sound is produced. The sound is made louder by a vocal sac which swells up like a huge bubble beneath the frog's chin.

▶ **A tree frog climbing down a tree at night.**

During the day, frogs stay hidden in shady places, where they are cool and moist. At night, they move around and begin to sing.

▲ A female (right) attracted by a male frog's croaking.

The female has tympanums, or ear membranes, located just below the eyes. When she hears the male's song, she comes near.

▲ A male on top of a female.

When the female comes close enough to be touched, the male climbs onto her back and holds on tight.

When a female comes near, the male frog climbs onto her back. He holds her by clasping her slippery body with his short, thick arms. The female is larger than the male and can easily carry him as she goes about, looking for a place to lay her eggs and catching insects.

Eventually, she hops into the water and eggs are released from her body. A female may lay a dozen eggs, or many thousands, depending on the species. The male discharges his sperm over the eggs, fertilizing them as they pass into the water. The eggs float on the water, encased in a jelly-like substance, which protects them.

▶ A tree frog's eggs.

Eggs are laid in a variety of ways, depending on the species of frog. Some float in spaghetti-like strings. Others may be in a mass. And still others are attached to underwater plants.

► **The male clings to this female as she lays her eggs.**

This species of tree frog lays five to thirty eggs at a time. It may lay a total of five hundred during one night.

▼ Tadpole embryos inside the egg cases. How fast the embryos develop depends on the temperature of the water and on the species of frog. Generally, the warmer the water, the faster the development.

▲ **The embryos' tails become visible.**

Within three days after these eggs were laid, the tails of the embryos become visible.

▲ **The tadpoles emerge.**

In about five days, these tadpoles have broken free of the egg case and begin life on their own in the water.

Because frog eggs are transparent, it is possible to see the changes that take place inside. The dark part of the egg, the animal pole, contains the speck that will develop into the frog. The light part, the vegetal pole, contains food for the developing embryo.

The cells begin to divide and the embryo grows very quickly. Soon a head, tail, and gills can be seen. Within several days, or weeks, depending on the species, all the embryos in the jelly mass begin to wriggle. Finally, they break free and begin the next phase of their lives, as tadpoles.

The development of a tadpole.

The cells multiply.   The embryo absorbs nutrition.   The tadpole's body forms.   The tadpole emerges.

● A tadpole developing into a frog (upper photos left to right.)

The tadpole eats heartily and grows rapidly. At first, its diet consists mainly of tiny bits of plant life, and it breathes with gills, like a fish. But eventually, the gills are replaced by lungs, and the tadpole begins to breathe oxygen from the air at the pond's surface. At the same time, its diet changes and it begins to eat mostly meat. As it grows, the tadpole's body becomes more frog-like. Its legs appear and it begins to swim with them. At the same time, the tadpole stops eating and begins to absorb its tail, which is rich in nutrients. All these changes are in preparation for the life it will live on land as an adult.

▶ A baby frog out of water.

By the time the tadpole's four legs have developed, its diet has changed and its lungs have developed. It is ready to leave the pond and begin life on land as a frog.

▲ Baby frogs climbing out of a pond.

These tiny frogs climb out of the water, clinging with their toes to the leaf of a water plant.

▲ A frog clinging to a leaf with its toes.

Tree frogs have pads on their fingers and toes. The pads act like suction cups, enabling them to easily cling to smooth leafy surfaces without slipping.

The tadpole and adult stages of a frog's life are so different, scientists call frogs "amphibians." *Amphibian* is a Greek word that means "two lives."

The dramatic physical change from tadpole to frog is called a metamorphosis. Except for its stubby tail, which will disappear in a few days, the transformation from tadpole to frog is complete when the frog comes out of the water to begin its life on land. Eventually the young frog will be ready to return to the water to mate. This may take a few months, or it may take a few years.

▼ A baby tree frog sitting on a leaf. This baby tree frog is less than an inch long. Although the baby frog resembles the adult frog, its body must still develop and mature.

◀ **A baby frog looking for prey.**

As soon as they leave the water, baby tree frogs begin catching live prey. They hop from leaf to leaf in search of all kinds of insects.

▶ **A frog aiming at an insect.**

When a frog spots a moving insect, it aims at it and jumps. Its tongue darts out with lightning speed to catch its prey and bring it inside its mouth.

Frogs are beneficial to people because they eat harmful insects—a variety of flies, beetles, and spiders. Frogs swallow their victims alive, without chewing them. They have long, sticky tongues which dart out with lightning speed to catch insects in flight. Sometimes the victim, a moth or cricket, may be almost as big as the tiny tree frog. Then the frog uses its hands to stuff its prey inside its mouth.

Their large, bulging eyes enable frogs to see behind and above themselves, as well as to the front and sides. Whenever something in its field of vision moves, the frog is instantly alerted and ready to strike.

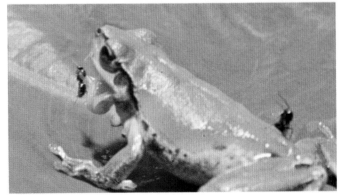

● **A tree frog eating an insect.**

If a frog catches a stinging insect, or one that doesn't taste good, it uses its fingers to pull the insect out of its mouth.

There are about five hundred species of tree frogs in the world. They have adapted to all kinds of climates. They can be found in the hardy Canadian woodlands or in lush tropical forests. In fact, tree frogs live everywhere except on the continent of Antarctica. About twenty-five species live in the United States. In the eastern part of the country, common species include the gray tree frog, the green tree frog, and the spring peeper.

Tree frogs are among the most colorful of frogs and are considered to be the best singers. Their padded feet, which other frogs do not have, make them extremely good climbers and jumpers.

◀ **A tree frog on a wildflower.**

Tree frogs live on blades of grass, on stems of wildflowers, and on tree trunks—wherever they can find insects. They return to the pond only in the spring in order to mate.

▶ **A parent and a baby frog.**

This baby frog rides on its mother's back. A fully grown tree frog of this species measures only an inch and a half long.

▲ A tree frog hanging from a leaf.

Tree frogs can cling to almost any surface. They can even hang upside down from a leaf or blade of grass.

▲ A tree frog holding onto a branch.

Tree frogs use their arms and legs to swing from branch to branch.

Tree frogs are the most acrobatic of the frogs. Their lightweight bodies and long, jointed legs make them agile climbers and jumpers. The strong hind legs are particularly well suited to jumping long distances. Tree frogs have special suction discs on their fingers and toes which help them keep their grip on even slippery surfaces. Most frogs have eight fingers and ten toes.

A tree frog's hands.

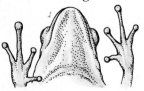

▶ A tree frog's jumping abilities.

This tree frog looks like a trapeze artist as it arches its back and stretches its legs during a long leap.

◀ Tree frogs blending in with the leaves.

These tree frogs remain still during the day and are hidden from enemies.

Tree frogs are hard to see because they blend in so well with their surroundings. Like many kinds of frogs, they can change the color of their skin. When they are hiding among tree leaves or grass, tree frogs turn bright green to match their background. If they are on the ground, or on tree bark, their skin color changes to brown. This ability to camouflage themselves helps tree frogs hide from enemies.

Scientists also think that frogs change the color of their skin in different kinds of weather. In hot temperatures, some species of frogs turn lighter in color. Their light skin reflects the sun's rays, and the frogs stay cooler. In cold weather, frogs may become darker. The dark color absorbs the sun's rays, and the frogs stay warmer.

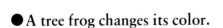

● A tree frog changes its color.

The three lower photos on page 22 and the photo on page 23 are of the same frog. Tree frogs protect themselves from enemies such as birds by changing their body color.

●**A tree frog waiting for prey.**

Tree frogs search for prey after dark. Some frogs wait near outdoor lights, which attract night-flying insects.

The frog's life is filled with danger at every stage of its development. Turtles, large fish, and wading birds are all hunters, or predators, of the tadpole. Tadpoles have few defenses except to move quickly away, or to burrow into the mud at the bottom of the pond to hide. Scientists guess that only one egg in twenty will become a frog, and that only one frog out of ten will live more than a year.

Snakes, bobcats, raccoons, and people all prey upon adult frogs. In addition to camouflaging themselves, some frogs protect themselves by puffing up their bodies to scare off enemies. Others secrete a poison that burns the mouths of their predators.

▶ A frog being swallowed by a snake.

Snakes are one of the frog's worst enemies. Snakes have a keen sense of smell and once they find a frog, they swallow it whole.

▼ A tree frog caught by a starling.

Most frogs die before they grow up because they are attacked by enemies or cannot find enough food to eat.

◄ **A black-horned katydid on a thistle.**

In fall, the sound of crickets and katydids replaces the chorus of singing frogs.

▶ **A tree frog in a grove in autumn.**

Because moisture evaporates quickly from their bodies, frogs must live in cool, damp places. Tree leaves provide frogs with shade and protection.

Frogs are cold-blooded animals. That means their body temperature changes with the temperature of the air. If the weather gets too hot, a frog's body will soon dry out and it will die. That is why frogs and toads usually hop about at night, or in shady places during the day. During times when the weather is very hot and dry, frogs may burrow underground and stay inactive for a time. This period of resting is called estivation.

The frog's skin is especially adapted to help keep it from drying out. Instead of drinking water, as people do, frogs can absorb water, or dew, through their skin. Frogs are constantly shedding their old skin, or molting. Some frogs molt every day, some just once a week. The old skin splits down the back, and the frog wriggles out of it, pulling it over its head. Then it eats the cast-off skin which is rich in nutrients.

◀ A tree in autumn.

▼ A tree frog sleeping underground.

The frog's body temperature changes according to the air temperature. In winter, the tree frog's body functions slow down, and it remains in an inactive state until spring.

▶ **A male tree frog singing in spring.**

As soon as the male frogs waken in the spring, they head for a nearby pond or stream. There, each one sings its own song to attract a mate. As the vocal sac swells beneath the frog's chin, its song becomes louder.

During the winter, frogs, like many other animals, go into hibernation. Their body functions slow down, and they go into a kind of sleep. Frogs burrow underground to stay warm during the long, cold winter. They seem to know instinctively how deep they must dig in order to be beneath the frost that will settle in the ground.

In spring, with the first rains of the year, the earth begins to warm up. Soon the frog awakens. Its heart begins to beat faster and its circulation speeds up. It needs air to breathe. So it digs its way out of the earth and immediately heads for a pond or stream where it will begin to sing its mating song.

Let's Find Out

Why Do Frogs Lay Their Eggs in Water?

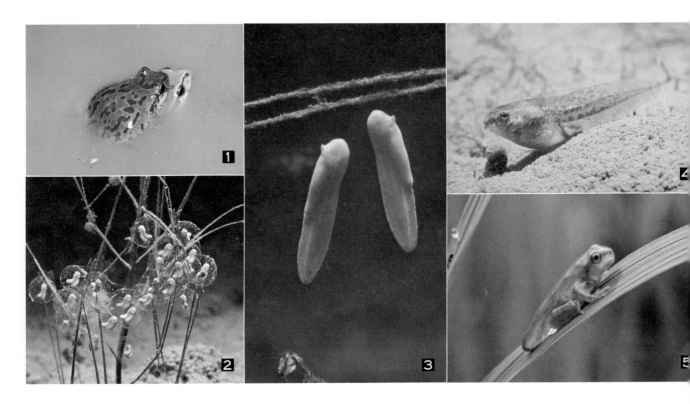

(1) A frog laying its eggs in water. (2) Frog embryos. (3) Tadpoles breathing through their gills. (4) A tadpole swimming, using its tail. (5) An infant frog coming out of the water.

salamander

A long time ago, frogs lived only in the water, and they belonged to the same family as salamanders. Eventually, frogs changed, and they began living on land. But because the eggs of frogs and other amphibians do not have shells, they are laid in the water to prevent them from drying out. The newly emerged tadpoles live in water until their bodies become ready to live on land. After their gills have been replaced by lungs, frogs come out of the water and begin their life on land.

Raising Tadpoles.

Fill a Container with Water.

If you use tap water, let the full container sit in the sun for several days. Then scoop some frog eggs from a pond. Place them in the container.

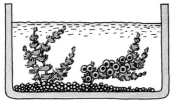

water plant

stones

water warmed in the sun

Gently scoop eggs from a pond. Carry them in a bucket or empty can.

Food for Tadpoles.

When tadpoles emerge from the eggs, feed them a small amount of bread crumbs or cooked rice. Do not overfeed them. When the water becomes dirty, change half of it. Feed the tadpoles dried fish from time to time.

bread crumbs

dried fish

cooked rice

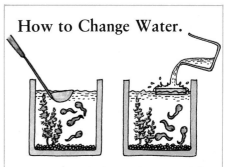

How to Change Water.

Use a soup ladle to dip out old water. Pour new water in gently, without making waves.

Place Stones in the Container.

When the legs of the tadpoles develop and their tails begin to shorten, take some water out of the container. Also add some stones. The baby frogs will climb out of the water onto the stones to begin breathing oxygen from the air.

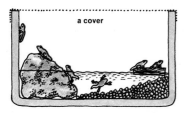

a cover

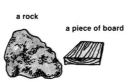

a rock

a piece of board

Food for Frogs.

Feed young frogs live plant lice and flies. Once the frogs have begun to eat, you should free them near a pond or a stream. Grown-up frogs are easier to keep. Feed them live flies and other insects.

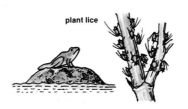

plant lice

flies

flies on spoiled food

GLOSSARY

cold-blooded animal—an animal whose temperature changes with the temperature of the air. (p. 26)

embryo—the early stages of development of a frog, toad, or other organism. (pp. 9, 10)

hibernation—a period of inactivity undergone by animals during cold weather when their body functions slow down. (pp. 4, 29)

instinct—behavior with which an animal is born, rather than behavior which is learned. (p. 29)

metamorphosis—a process of development during which dramatic physical changes take place. Frogs go through three stages: egg, tadpole, and adult. (p. 14)

predators—animals that hunt and kill other animals for food. (p. 24)

prey—animals that are killed by predators. (pp. 16, 24)

species—A group of animals which scientists have identified as having common traits. (pp. 4, 6, 19)

tympanums—ear membranes. (p. 8)

vocal sac—an elastic skin sac beneath the frog's chin, which swells up to amplify the sound as a frog sings. (pp. 6, 29)